Put Beginning Readers on the Right Track with
ALL ABOARD READING™

The All Aboard Reading series is especially designed for beginning readers. Written by noted authors and illustrated in full color, these are books that children really want to read—books to excite their imagination, expand their interests, make them laugh, and support their feelings. With fiction and nonfiction stories that are high interest and curriculum-related, All Aboard Reading books offer something for every young reader. And with four different reading levels, the All Aboard Reading series lets you choose which books are most appropriate for your children and their growing abilities.

Picture Readers
Picture Readers have super-simple texts, with many nouns appearing as rebus pictures. At the end of each book are 24 flash cards—on one side is a rebus picture; on the other side is the written-out word.

Station Stop 1
Station Stop 1 books are best for children who have just begun to read. Simple words and big type make these early reading experiences more comfortable. Picture clues help children to figure out the words on the page. Lots of repetition throughout the text helps children to predict the next word or phrase—an essential step in developing word recognition.

Station Stop 2
Station Stop 2 books are written specifically for children who are reading with help. Short sentences make it easier for early readers to understand what they are reading. Simple plots and simple dialogue help children with reading comprehension.

Station Stop 3
Station Stop 3 books are perfect for children who are reading alone. With longer text and harder words, these books appeal to children who have mastered basic reading skills. More complex stories captivate children who are ready for more challenging books.

In addition to All Aboard Reading books, look for All Aboard Math Readers™ (fiction stories that teach math concepts children are learning in school) and All Aboard Science Readers™ (nonfiction books that explore the most fascinating science topics in age-appropriate language).

All Aboard for happy reading!

To my friend Ting—E.N.

To Terry—C.R.

Library of Congress Cataloging-in-Publication Data

Neye, Emily.
    Water / by Emily Neye ; illustrated by Cindy Revell.
      p. cm. — (All aboard science reader. Station stop 1)
    Summary: Describes the sources, uses, and properties of water.
    1. Water—Juvenile literature. [1. Water.] I. Revell, Cindy, ill. II. Title. III. Series.
  GB662.3 .N49 2002
  553.7—dc21

                                              2002007507

ISBN 0-448-42847-4 (pbk)   A B C D E F G H I J

ISBN 0-448-42878-4 (GB)   A B C D E F G H I J

Water

By Emily Neye
Illustrated by Cindy Revell

Grosset & Dunlap • New York

Water is all around us.

4

Water can be many things.

Water is rain from the sky.

Water is a puddle
on the ground.

Water is a place to swim.
It is a clear pond.

It is waves in the ocean.

Water is for drinking.

Water is for cooking.

Water is for cleaning.

But that is not all.

When the air gets cold,
drops of water turn to snow.

When water gets cold,
it gets hard.

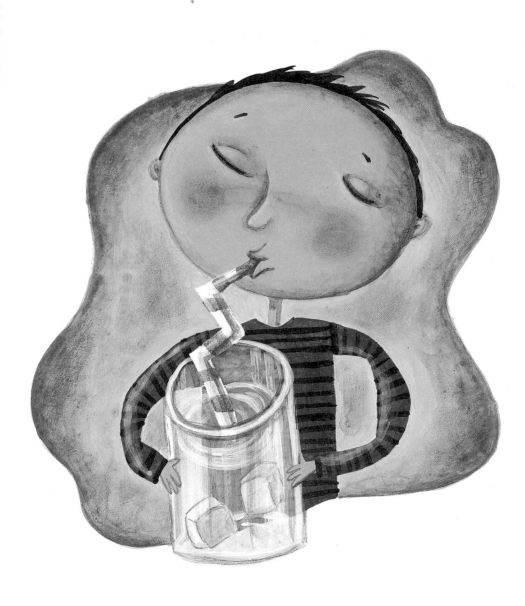

It is ice cubes
in your drink.

It is ice to skate on.

It is icicles to lick.

But water can change.

The sun shines down.

The water turns soft.

It drips and drips.

Now the water is
on the ground.

It is a lake.

It is a stream.

It is water in a well.

But water can change.

When water gets very hot,
it steams and steams.

Now the water is in the air.

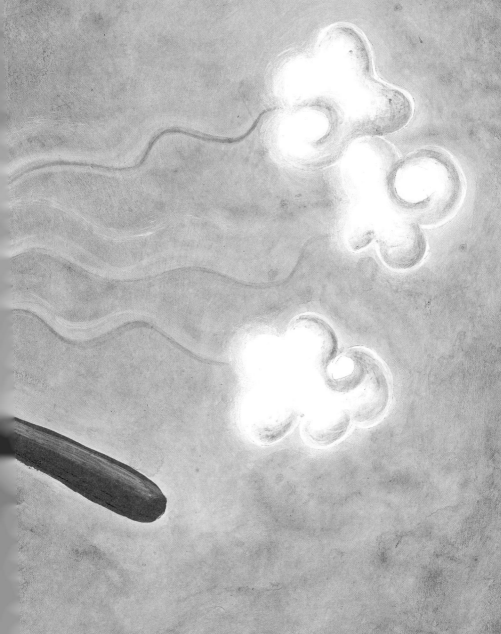

24

Steam is tiny drops
of water floating in the air.

A cloud is also tiny drops
of water floating in the air.

But the water does not float
in the air for long.

It gets heavy.

It falls down to the ground.

We call it rain.

Rain or snow,

ice or steam,

it is all water.

Water can be many things.

And water can be fun!